FIFTEEN SHADES

OF

LOVE

BIBLE STUDY FOR WOMEN SERIES (SPECIAL)

Kimberly Taylor

TakeBackYourTemple.com

Cover Image by:

www.iStockphoto.com

Table of Contents

Introduction

The human heart's deepest need is for love. While real love is becoming rarer by the day, it still exists. In this book, I'll show you what real love is (and is not) according to the bible. You will learn about the qualities of a loving person and how to develop them.

You'll discover how to love another person as God loves you and see how good that can be. Love at its best is about *restoration:* You see another's flaws and scars - and love them anyway.

As you apply yourself to learning about genuine love, you will never settle for a counterfeit.

When I was a teenager, I got my ideas about what love is like from romance novels. I devoured them by the case. These novels took me away to lands where the heroes were noble, true, and protective - even risking their lives to save their heroines. While I enjoyed the books, they left me with longing when I compared them with reality.

If only...

What I experienced in relationships as a single adult was a far cry from the romance novels. I discovered that many of the men I attracted weren't noble or true. The relationships I had, mostly based on sex, left me empty, damaged, and insecure emotionally. Not to mention the damage *I caused* from acting contrary to God's word.

That is what happens when you settle for the counterfeit!

A book called *Fifty Shades of Grey* is currently topping the bestseller lists. Out of curiosity, I read the synopsis and discovered that it is about the sexual bondage relationship between two young adults.

I was surprised to learn that *women* are the book's primary buyers. A reviewer speculated that, beyond the sexual content, the book speaks to a woman's desire for love.

That desire is a manifestation of what Jesus said would happen in the latter days before His return: "And because lawlessness will abound, the love of many will grow cold (Matthew 24:12)."

Don't we see that every day? As this world strives to take God out of it, the love people have for one another deteriorates. Criminal acts, injustice, and abuse abounds. Like outer space is cold and dark without the warmth and light of the sun, so is the human heart without the love of the **Son**, Jesus Christ.

1 John 1:5 says of Him: "This is the message which we have heard from Him and declare to you, that God is light and in Him is no darkness at all."

It is ironic to me that the main male character in *Fifty Shades of Grey* is named *Christian*

Grey. But with our Lord and Savior *Jesus Christ*, there are no shades of gray in His love. Certainly there isn't darkness!

In Him, there is only light. Jesus invites us to walk in the warmth and security of His love every day.

I experienced Jesus' love for the first time back in 2001.

That year, I attended a Christian women's conference to support a friend going through a tough time. I didn't want to be there. Little did I know God had other plans for me!

You see, I never knew a man's love, protection, and security. My father had abandoned our family when I was a baby. But during that women's conference, the event coordinators had created a theme called "The Father/Daughter Dinner" on a Saturday night. When we arrived, the dining room was decorated like a prom with corsages at every place setting and a silver ring.

They also had a letter written "from God" (based upon biblical scripture) to His precious daughters about how much He loved them. The letter touched my heart as I learned how God desired to have a personal relationship with me.

I lost it. I cried at that dinner more than I have ever cried outside of a funeral!

Then, the ladies had another surprise. They had men to come in to pray for us – husbands, fathers, friends. These men also sang praise songs and we all worshipped the Lord together.

Then they prayed for us. In the prayer, they apologized for not being the men God called them to be. They pledged to protect us as precious women of God.

Through that one event, God healed the hurt, anger, and grief inside of me. He revealed Himself to me as a loving, protective Father. I have never been the same.

I discovered that the kind of love God has for his people is *Agape* love, which is a Greek word translated as "a commitment of the will to cherish and uphold another." This is loving someone regardless of how you feel; it is loving someone apart from how they treat you.

When I received God's *Agape* love, all the **gaps** inside of me were filled. His love made me whole. His love promised to uphold me no matter what I was going through.

Every day, I am discovering new aspects of God's view of love. He spells it out in 1 Corinthians 13:4-8:

> *Love suffers long and is kind; love does not envy; love does not parade itself, is not puffed up; does not behave rudely, does not seek its own, is not provoked, thinks no evil; does not rejoice in iniquity, but rejoices in the truth; bears all things, believes all things, hopes all things, endures all things. Love never fails.*

Because God loves me, I am now free to love myself. Jesus commands us to love our neighbors *as ourselves* (see Matthew 22:39). The operative word is **as** which is interpreted 'to the degree of'.

God expects you to love yourself according to this scripture. This tells me that you are limited in your ability to love others if you aren't able to receive God's love and love yourself.

Jesus makes it plain in John 13:34-35: "A new commandment I give to you, that you love one another; as I have loved you, that you also love one another. By this all will know that you are My disciples, if you have love for one another."

If you have any barriers that are keeping you from fully receiving God's love and loving yourself, then I recommend you pray for God to heal your heart immediately. As a motivational speaker once said, "If you miss love, you miss life."

Because you are reading a bible study, I assume that you already have a relationship with God through accepting Jesus Christ as your Savior. But in case, the following resource shows you how to establish a relationship with God through Jesus Christ or use it as a means to re-dedicate your life to Christ:

http://www.everystudent.com/features/ gettingconnected.html

Are you ready to learn more about real love as defined in the bible? We are going to uncover the treasures in 1 Corinthians 13:4-8. This study is longer than the other *Bible Study for Women* series guides because I needed more than 4 weeks to cover these scriptures. Let's get started!

How to Get the Most from this Study

The aim for each study in the *Bible Study for Women* series is to keep it simple. I want the lessons in the bible to change your life. To that end, it should be helpful to know how the lessons are organized and what you need to make the most of your study time.

Within each week's lesson, you will find:

- *Focus scriptures* to memorize related to the current topic

- *Lesson Insight* that discusses the week's story in depth

- *Speak the WORD* affirmations that confirm your identity in Christ

- *Aim for Change* that provides questions for further reflection and discussion

To start the study, you need to have:

- *A bible:* I recommend the *New King James Version* or the *New American Standard Bible* for readability. I believe that it is important to use a bible translation that you understand for private study.

- *Index cards:* These will come in handy to write focus scriptures on so that you can 'feed' on them throughout the day.

- *A small notebook or journal:* This will enable you to keep track of the blessings/lessons you are learning as a result of this study.

- *A heart and mind that is open to the Holy Spirit's teaching:* One of the Holy Spirit's roles in the believer's life is that of *Teacher* (John 14:26). Invite Him through prayer to show you plainly the lesson God wants to teach you before you begin each study session. Be attentive to the still small voice within that prompts you to take action on the word you are learning about.

- *A commitment and willingness to give yourself grace:* If you find yourself forgetting to study as you planned, don't beat yourself up. Just start your study where you left off at your next opportunity. Think "forward motion" and keep going!

Week 1: Love Suffers Long

Focus scripture

"But I say to you, love your enemies, bless those who curse you, do good to those who hate you, and pray for those who spitefully use you and persecute you, that you may be sons of your Father in heaven;"

- Matthew 5:44-45

Lesson Insight

Boy did I fight this lesson title! You see, in another version of I Corinthians 13:4, it said that *Love is patient.* But when I read it recently in the New King James version, it says *Love suffers long*.

What? Who wants to suffer? Isn't love all hearts and flowers like the romance novels and greeting card industry portrays it?

Not always...in fact, not most of the time! Love happens in the midst of *life*, and life is full of problems. In addition, relationships involve people and people aren't perfect. There is always the potential for conflict, anger, bruised feelings, and misunderstandings.

Because those things hurt, you suffer when they occur.

You can also suffer in *responding Godly* when those things happen to you. As the Focus scripture says, you are exhorted to:

- Love your enemies
- Bless those who curse you
- Do good to those who hate you
- Pray for those who spitefully use you and persecute you

I don't know about you, but my flesh doesn't want to do that! My natural self wants to hurt those who hurt me. And yet, I'm reminded again of God's *Agape* love for me: "a commitment of the will to cherish and uphold another."

I often remind myself: "It's a commitment of the *will*, not a commitment of the feel!" You make up your mind to do what pleases God, no matter what. You resolve to wait patiently for people, praying for them and trusting that God will continue to work on them.

God is our ultimate role-model for suffering long. In my opinion, there isn't a greater book in the bible that demonstrates God's long-suffering than the book of Judges. In this book, you'll see the same frustrating cycle repeated in almost every chapter:

1. The children of Israel did evil in the sight of the Lord.
2. The Lord delivered them into the hands of an enemy.
3. The children of Israel cried out to the Lord for deliverance.

4. The Lord in His compassion raised up a Judge to deliver the people.
5. After deliverance and a few years of obedience, the people once again did evil in the sight of the Lord...

The story of the children of Israel in Judges 10:6-18 is the perfect example.

It starts out badly: "Then the children of Israel again did evil in the sight of the Lord, and served the Baals and the Ashtoreths, the gods of Syria, the gods of Sidon, the gods of Moab, the gods of the people of Ammon, and the gods of the Philistines; and they forsook the Lord and did not serve Him. (verse 6)"

These false gods were detestable to God; the people who worshipped them engaged in sexual immorality, consorting with male and female temple prostitutes. Some of the rituals to these gods even required child sacrifice!

How did the children of Israel end up degrading themselves with idol worship after the Lord had done so much good for them? He delivered them out of Egyptian slavery, performed miracles such as the Red Sea crossing, brought water out of a rock for them, and fed them with manna in the desert.

God also kept his promise in bringing them into the Promised Land, a land described as overflowing with "milk and honey." So it certainly wasn't anything the Lord did to provoke the Israelites to worship false gods. Rather, it was their own disobedience.

When the children of Israel were commanded to go into the Promised Land, God told them to dispossess the previous inhabitants. But they didn't do it.

Instead, they allowed some of the inhabitants to stay. Instead of the Israelites converting the inhabitants to worship the one True God, they were influenced by them to turn away from God. They compromised their beliefs to fit in with them. Sounds like what is happening to this nation, doesn't it?

The children of Israel ended up enslaved because of their error - literally. The Lord sold them into the hand of the Philistines and Ammonites. These were the very people whose gods the Israelites had called upon as their masters and owners.

However after 18 years, the children of Israel came to their senses. They called upon the Lord once again and confessed their sin.

Notice the Lord's response in Judges 10:11-14: "...Did I not deliver you from the Egyptians and from the Amorites and from the people of Ammon and from the Philistines? Also the Sidonians and Amalekites and Maonites oppressed you; and you cried out to Me, and I delivered you from their hand. Yet you have forsaken Me and served other gods. Therefore I will deliver you no more. Go and cry out to the gods which you have chosen; let them deliver you in your time of distress."

Can you hear the Lord's frustration? He says that he had delivered them from five nations previously and yet, they ended up returning to those same nation's gods!

It is unfortunate, but many of us can relate to the Israelite's behavior. God delivers us from a destructive relationship or an addictive behavior. We enjoy freedom for a while but then the past calls us again. We start remembering the "good times" of sin and forget about the "steal, kill, and destroy" part.

And when you trade a lie for the truth, you end up in bondage.

Continuing the story, the Lord challenged the Israelites to cry out to the false gods to whom they had returned and see how much help they received.

I am sure that the Israelites probably went to the false gods first and when that didn't work, they remembered the one true God.

The Israelites took an admirable step next; they backed up confession of their sin with action. They put away the foreign gods and served the Lord.

After that, the scriptures says something very telling about the Lord's love: "And His soul could no longer endure the misery of Israel."

This tells me the Lord has empathy for us. He doesn't like to see us endure unnecessary suffering.

I think it is important to point out long-suffering does not mean enduring abuse. As you will see in the upcoming chapters, abuse is not part of love.

You don't have to form close relationships with or trust untrustworthy people. The bible says that we must have discernment in our dealings with others; according to Matthew 10:16, we should be harmless as doves, but wise as serpents.

We recognize that we love people because we see them as souls that God created for a purpose and love them as an act of obedience to Christ. But we do not have to like everyone's *ways*.

It is wise to separate ourselves from people who deliberately harm us emotionally or physically. You can uphold those people in prayer if they don't know Jesus. And you can commit to treating them kindly, even if they aren't kind to you.

That is a much more powerful testimony to them than returning evil for their evil. The world does that. But we are called to stand out, not fit in. Our love enables us to shine in a dark world and will became even more important as the world gets darker.

Speak the WORD

Speak this affirmation out loud as often as possible, based on this week's study:

> "Lord, thank you for teaching me to love as you love through the people I meet.

Through the guidance of your Holy Spirit, I am slow to anger, quick to forgive, and I pray for those with whom I have conflicts. Lord, help me to be long-suffering with people's faults, just as you are long-suffering with mine."

Aim For Change

Read Judges 10: 6-18 and then answer the following questions.

1. In what way did the Israelites do evil in the sight of the Lord?

2. How did the Lord respond to the Israelites behavior?

3. What did the Israelites do to show repentance?

4. When the Israelites repented, what does the scripture say about the Lord's response?

5. Think about the people in your life; how can you demonstrate patience with them when their conduct is less than stellar?

Week 2: Love is Kind

Focus scripture

> *"Therefore, whatever you want men to do to you, do also to them, for this is the Law and the Prophets."*

- Matthew 7:12

Lesson Insight

Do you remember the Golden Rule that your elders taught you? They said, "Do unto others as you would have them do unto you." I am sure that you want others to be kind to you, so you can set the example and be kind to them first!

What does it mean to be kind? To be kind to someone is to be courteous, gentle, and gracious. It is treating other people with respect. When you think about it, it goes right along with the concept of long-suffering – especially when the other person isn't kind to you. Notice the principle is to "do unto others as you *would have them do* unto you," not "do unto others as *they are doing* unto you!"

When you allow other's poor treatment of you to influence how you treat them, then you are turning your power over to them. You become like waves in the ocean, letting the wind toss you to and fro. However, when you commit to following God's word, it becomes an anchor to you, keeping you sure and steadfast.

When you treat others kindly in spite of how they treat you, that is your opportunity to demonstrate the excellence of our faith.

Jesus taught this principle in Luke 6:32-35. He said: "But if you love those who love you, what credit is that to you? For even sinners love those who love them. And if you do good to those who do good to you, what credit is that to you? For even sinners do the same. And if you lend to those from whom you hope to receive back, what credit is that to you? For even sinners lend to sinners to receive as much back. But love your enemies, do good, and lend, hoping for nothing in return; and your reward will be great, and you will be sons of the Most High. For He is kind to the unthankful and evil."

Wow! That is indeed a high standard, but we can do it as we submit to the power of the Holy Spirit that lives within us. Love is not only a feeling; it is an action. Showing kindness to others is love in action.

We are also instructed in the greatest commandment that we should love our neighbors as ourselves. This is not a conditional statement as in, "We should love our neighbors as ourselves, as long as they love us." No, our commitment to love others and be kind to them is independent of what they do or say. We do it to imitate our Father as His dear children.

Nowhere in the Bible is kindness demonstrated more vividly than in the parable Jesus told in Luke 10:25-37, the parable of the good Samaritan.

Jesus told a parable in response to a lawyer's question: "Teacher, what shall I do to inherit eternal life?" The man asked Jesus the question to test him.

However, Jesus asked him a question in return, asking him what the law said about it.

The man answered: "You shall love the Lord your God with all your heart, with all your soul, with all your strength, and with all your mind,' and 'your neighbor as yourself.'"

Jesus responded to him: "...You have answered rightly; do this and you will live (verses 27-28)."

I don't think the importance of this statement can be overstated; we know that Jesus died to give us life in abundance. But do we really know what the essence of life is?

John 17:3 defines life: "And this is eternal life, that they may know You, the only true God, and Jesus Christ whom You have sent."

Life is about our relationship with God. It is that simple and that complex!

We are commanded to love God, but one way we are called to demonstrate our love for God is how we treat our neighbor. In the scripture, we see that the lawyer was looking for a loophole in verse 29 when he asked Jesus, "And who is my neighbor?" The scripture says that he asked the question in order to justify himself.

So that was the set up: Now let's get into the meat of the story.

"A certain man went down from Jerusalem to Jericho, and fell among thieves, who stripped him of his clothing, wounded him, and departed, leaving him half dead. Now by chance a certain priest came down that road. And when he saw him, he passed by on the other side.

Likewise a Levite, when he arrived at the place, came and looked, and passed by on the other side (verses 30-31)."

The injured man clearly needed help, but the priest and a Levite ignored his pain and passed him by. Notice that these were religious men in the Jewish faith; you would think that they would know the law but there is a difference between knowing the law and practicing the law.

But a certain Samaritan, as he journeyed, came where he was. And when he saw him, he had compassion. So he went to him and bandaged his wounds, pouring on oil and wine; and he set him on his own animal, brought him to an inn, and took care of him. On the next day, when he departed, he took out two denarii, gave them to the innkeeper, and said to him, 'Take care of him; and whatever more you spend, when I come again, I will repay you (verses 33-35).'

The Samaritan's response indicates an important component of kindness: He had compassion for the man's condition.

Compassion is the ability to identify with another's situation. The Samaritan recognized the man's need and did what he could to meet it. Not only did he meet the man's current need, but he went the extra mile and provided money to the innkeeper to meet the man's future needs.

At the end of the story, Jesus asked his questioner, "So which of these three do you think was neighbor to him who fell among the thieves?"

The man answered, "He who showed mercy on him."

Jesus responded, "Go and do likewise." Not only was He talking to the lawyer, but it is a charge to each one of us through his Word.

Compassion. Grace. Forgiveness. All of these characteristics are components of kindness. Imitate your Father in heaven and do as He does.

Speak the WORD

Speak this affirmation out loud as often as possible, based on this week's study:

> "Father, I want to be like you! You are not only kind to Your children, but you are kind to the unthankful and evil. I am thankful that you teach me to do the same in Your Word. I subdue my fleshly nature and allow the Holy Spirit's power to work through me. You said that you can do exceeding, abundantly, above all that I can ask or think according to the power that works in me. I allow that power free course in my life so that I glorify you when I am kind to others."

Aim For Change

Read Matthew 7:12, Luke 6:32-35, and Luke 10:25-37 and then answer the following questions.

1. How does scripture say that we should treat others?

2. Should how others treat us influence how we should treat them? Why or why not?

3. What did Jesus say was the result of treating others regardless of how they treat you?

4. In the parable of the good Samaritan, how did the Levite and priest respond to the injured man?

5. How did the Samaritan respond to the injured man?

6. What character traits did the Samaritan demonstrate in his actions?

7. How can you demonstrate kindness to those you meet going forward?

Week 3: Love Does Not Envy

Focus scripture

"Let your conduct be without covetousness; be content with such things as you have. For He Himself has said, "I will never leave you nor forsake you."

- Hebrews 13:5

Lesson Insight

In the first two weeks of our study, we discussed what love is. In the coming weeks, we will review what love is not.

In 1 Corinthians 13, we are told that love does not envy. What is so bad about envy? First, let's define what envy is. Envy is defined as "a feeling of discontent or covetousness with regard to another's advantages, success, and possessions."

Envy is different from jealousy; while jealousy wants an item just like that which another person owns, envy wants to *take* what another person has. Envy has no regard for another person's rights. It disturbs your peace and leaves you unhappy.

Envy comes from "zero sum thinking" – you can't be happy when someone else succeeds because you erroneously believe that there is not enough to go around.

In 1 Kings 21, you see envy taken to the extreme. Ahab, the King of Samaria, wanted his neighbor's vineyard. He said that he wanted the vineyard because he wanted to plant a vegetable garden that was within walking distance to his palace.

But the neighbor, Naboth, refuse to sell the vineyard because it had been in his family for generations.

The King had a moping fit. He became depressed, lay down on his bed, and refused to eat. Sounds like a little child, doesn't it? His wife came to him, and basically asked him what was the matter with him.

Now I have to pause the story, and tell you who his wife was: Her name was Jezebel. Did you shudder? It is amazing that the very name is associated with bad things. So now that you know that she is involved in this story, you know that something bad is going to happen!

King Ahab told Jezebel what had happened with Naboth and she took charge. She told her husband that he could get up, eat, and be happy because she was going to give him Naboth's vineyard.

Jezebel concocted a truly evil scheme: She sent letters in Ahab's name to the city elders and nobles. The letters directed these nobles to proclaim a fast, pretending that they were going to honor him. They were to have him seated between two criminals, who would lie and say that he had blasphemed against God and the king. The natural result of this false accusation was that poor Naboth would be stoned to death.

Things happened exactly the way Jezebel planned; Naboth was stoned and killed. She reported to her husband that Naboth was dead and he could now have the vineyard. Was King Ahab appalled that his wife had done such a despicable thing to get what he wanted. No! Without a moment's remorse, he took possession of Naboth's vineyard. But don't worry; in the later chapters, you discover that both King Ahab and Jezebel paid the price for their evil acts.

Now you might think, "I would never murder someone to take what they have." But envy begins in the heart. Remember how Jesus said that if a man looks at a women with lust, he has already committed adultery with her in his heart (see Matthew 5:27-28)? That same principle can be applied when we lust after other people's possessions.

It causes you to resent the other person and that resentment will affect how you treat them.

Instead, we are exhorted to be content with the things we have. Does that mean that you can't want more? No, but contentment means that you maintain a state of peaceful happiness with what you have in the meantime. You truly enjoy what you have, recognizing that it all comes to you from God's generous hand.

When you are content, it is easier to be generous with others. Instead of you seeing God as a God of scarcity, you believe that He supplies all of your needs according to His riches and glory by Christ Jesus.

With that attitude, you can truly be happy when other people are blessed, knowing that your turn is coming.

Speak the WORD

Speak this affirmation out loud as often as possible, based on this week's study:

"Lord, I am content with what you have given me. Thank you for your generosity and your care for me. Whenever I experience thoughts of jealousy about what someone else has, I take those thoughts captive to the obedience of Jesus Christ immediately. I am able to be happy when others are blessed, knowing that I have already received the most precious gift - my Salvation purchased with the precious blood of Jesus."

Aim For Change

Read 1 Kings 21. Then answer the following questions.

1. What did Naboth have that King Ahab wanted?

2. Why did King Ahab want it?

3. How did King Ahab respond when Naboth refused his offer?

4. When Ahab told Jezebel what happened, how did she respond?

5. What plan did Jezebel devise to acquire Naboth's possession?

6. Why do you think envy is a barrier to loving another person?

7. Think about your current level of contentment with your possessions. Do you often compare what you have with what others have? Do you covet what another person has? If so, take a moment to thank the Lord for your possessions and ask Him in prayer for help to take envious thoughts captive the obedience of Christ.

Week 4: Love Does Not Parade Itself

Focus scripture

*A man's pride will bring him low,
But the humble in spirit will retain
honor*

- Proverbs 29:23

Lesson Insight

Think about the word "Parade" for a moment. What images come to mind? I know when I think of it, I see images that are loud, bold, and larger than life. A parade calls attention to itself; its whole purpose is "look at me!"

When I read the focus scripture, I immediately thought about how Satan was described in the Old Testament. He was the epitome of the "look at me" attitude. In Isaiah 14:12-15, his original name, Lucifer, was used in describing his rebellion against God. See if you can spot the parading attitude in his statements:

"...'I will ascend into heaven,

I will exalt my throne above the stars of God;

I will also sit on the mount of the congregation

On the farthest sides of the north;

I will ascend above the heights of the clouds,

I will be like the Most High.' (Isaiah 14:13-14)"

In the parading attitude, it's all about you and exalting yourself. You want to put yourself and your needs above everyone else! That is not love.

Satan's motive was to ascend to a high place so that he could be worshiped like God. But, as a disciple of Christ your motive is not "look at me," but "look at Him." You want others to see the Christ in you so that they too will accept him as their Savior and be drawn into a personal relationship with Him.

The bible commends a humble attitude. My pastor once defined humility as not thinking less of yourself, but thinking of yourself *less*. You see yourself as God sees you, which is the proper perspective. And because you love Him, you think of how you can accomplish God's agenda more than you think about your own agenda.

You can see the outcome of a prideful, parading attitude in Lucifer's outcome verse Isaiah 14:15: "Yet you shall be brought down to Sheol, To the lowest depths of the Pit." The parading attitude will bring you down to Satan's level!

Let's review another situation in which the desire to parade oneself brought about a destructive end. In Acts Chapter 4, we see love in action among the New Testament believers:

"Now the multitude of those who believed were of one heart and one soul; neither did anyone say that any of the things he possessed was his own, but they had all things in common. And with great power the apostles gave witness to the resurrection of the Lord Jesus. And great grace was upon them all. Nor was there anyone among them who lacked; for all who were possessors of lands or houses sold them, and brought the proceeds of the things that were sold, and laid them at the apostles' feet; and they distributed to each as anyone had need (Acts 4:32-35).

One believer, Joses, was commended because he sold his land, brought the money from the proceeds and laid it at the apostles' feet.

Unfortunately, this fact sparked a deceptive plan in the hearts of a couple in that same congregation: Ananias and Sapphira (see Acts 5:1-11). They decided to sell a possession as Joses had done, but they kept back part of the proceeds. However, they gave the impression that they were giving all and laid the remaining amount at the apostles' feet.

However the apostle Peter, given knowledge by the Holy Spirit of what they had done, confronted them: "Ananias, why has Satan filled your heart to lie to the Holy Spirit and keep back part of the price of the land for yourself? While it remained, was it not your own? And after it was sold, was it not in your own control? Why have you conceived this thing in your heart? You have not lied to men but to God (verses 3-4)."

Peter's insight tells me that Ananias' and Sapphira's motive in selling the possession and bringing it to the apostles was not helping to provide for their fellow believers out of love, but was just for public recognition. Again, their motive was "look at me" not "look at God."

When Ananias heard that his plan was exposed, he fell down dead. It appears that he had some serious heart problems! Now, I have no way of knowing if the man had heart problems from a physical perspective, but he certainly had heart problems from a spiritual one.

The scriptures tell us that about three hours later his wife came in, not knowing that her husband was dead. The apostle Peter asked her to confirm the amount that the possession was sold for, apparently because that was the amount that Ananias had told him.

Unfortunately, Sapphira revealed that she was part of the deceptive plan by agreeing that the amount her husband had told Peter was the truth.

Just as at the first, Peter stated that the offense was not committed against man but against God. In Ananias's case, Peter characterized it as lying to the Holy Spirit, to God. In Sapphira's case, he characterized it as testing the Holy Spirit. We know that the Holy Spirit knows all things. He has the ability to discern our motives and the intents of our heart.

In dramatic fashion, Sapphira also fell down dead when the apostle Peter called her out. They buried her by her husband. Scripture records that great fear came upon all who heard the story. So you see, the couple received the recognition they were seeking, just not in the manner that they intended!

This story has much to teach us. Whenever we are serving others, we should always take personal inventory to determine if we are doing it out of real concern or for public recognition. If for public recognition, that points to the fact that you are attempting to derive your value from what man thinks about you rather than what God thinks about you.

The desire for man's approval can lead you into deception and compromising your values, just as it did with Ananias and Sapphira. But when you are fully able to receive God's love for you, then you are able to serve others from the spirit of love and generosity.

Your actions will then put the spotlight on where it belongs: The goodness of our God!

Speak the WORD

Speak this affirmation out loud as often as possible, based on this week's study:

My God, how great you are! I am
grateful that you chose to love me before
I was even conceived. Help me not to
think higher of myself than I ought.
When I serve others, revealed the
motives of my heart if they are not pure.
I invite the cleansing power of Jesus'
blood to wash away impure motives.
Make all my actions those that bring
glory to you. You are worthy of all
praise!

Aim For Change

Read Acts 4:32-35 and Acts 5:1-11 and then
answer the following questions.

1. What did Joses do?

2. What do you think his motive was?

3. What did Ananias and Sapphira do?

4. Why do you think they kept back part of
   the proceeds?

5. Why do you think the apostle Peter characterized the couple's actions as lying to and testing the Holy Spirit?

6. What was the ultimate outcome for Ananias and Sapphira?

7. Are you currently rendering service to others in your church or community? Take a moment to think about your motive. Is the primary force behind your actions to glorify God, or to bring attention to yourself? If your motive is the latter, then ask God in prayer to cleanse your motive so that it be pure in His sight and that your service help others to see Him in action.

Week 5: Love is Not Puffed Up

Focus scripture

For I say, through the grace given to me, to everyone who is among you, not to think of himself more highly than he ought to think, but to think soberly, as God has dealt to each one a measure of faith.

- Romans 12:3

Lesson Insight

What is a parade without a big balloon full of hot air? That is the mental image I get when I think of a puffed up person. It makes me want to get a straight pin and prick them, just to let some of the air out!

I think a major danger that we need to guard against is forgetting that the Lord is the source of everything we are and everything we have. There are two areas in which we are vulnerable here: our Spiritual gifts and our material possessions.

God has given me the gift of teaching and writing. I have learned to go on "high alert" within myself whenever someone complements me on those gifts. I am very careful to reflect the glory back to God. I treat it like throwing a monkey off my back because I know the minute I start believing my own press, I am in trouble. Pride will try to take over my heart and I'll start thinking these gifts originate with me rather than God.

This in turn would create separation from God and, because I see myself as higher than others, it would negatively impact my ability to love them.

Getting puffed up reminds me of a scene from the movie "Superman" from the 1970s. In the scene, Superman takes Lois Lane flying with Him. At first, she is terrified and holds onto him for dear life. Eventually though, she starts getting comfortable with being airborne. She loosens her death grip on him and he holds her up with an arm around her. Then, she starts to inch herself away from his body until she is holding onto his arm, then just his hand.

You can see the mental progression as Lois begins to think that she is the one flying. Eventually, she is just hanging on to Superman by her fingertips. Then, disaster! Her fingertips slip off of his and she begins plummeting to the Earth, screaming.

But Superman, faster than a speeding bullet, flies to her rescue and bears her up again.

That scene reminds me that the only way I can "fly" and operate in my gifts is if the Lord bears me up. Lois' mistake was trying to separate herself from Superman. She started to value the flying more than the relational closeness she received from flying with him.

My heart's cry is this: "Lord, I want to fly with you. I want to see your awesome wonders. I want to experience your mighty deeds. I don't want to fly by myself. Bear me up on your mighty wings so that I can feel the warm and security of your love always."

In Jeremiah 13:11, we are told God's vision of His relationship with His people: "For as the sash clings to the waist of a man, so I have caused the whole house of Israel and the whole house of Judah to cling to Me,' says the Lord, 'that they may become My people, for renown, for praise, and for glory; but they would not hear.'"

And here is another statement of God's relationship vision: "...that you may love the Lord your God, that you may obey His voice, and that you may cling to Him, for He is your life and the length of your days; (Deuteronomy 30:20)"

Have you ever heard the complaint about yourself or you've said it about another, "You're too clingy"? But God will never say that; He wants us to be "clingy" with Him! The more you cling to Him and derive your worth from Him, the less dependent you become on other people's opinions.

The closer you cling to God, the more you'll be able to love others the way He loves you. You'll be learning from the Master!

Let's take a look at another way we can become too puffed up: Deriving our importance from material possessions.

The children of Israel were warned about this in Deuteronomy 8:11-14: "Beware that you do not forget the Lord your God by not keeping His commandments, His judgments, and His statutes which I command you today, lest— when you have eaten and are full, and have built beautiful houses and dwell in them; and when your herds and your flocks multiply, and your silver and your gold are multiplied, and all that you have is multiplied; when your heart is lifted up, and you forget the Lord your God who brought you out of the land of Egypt, from the house of bondage;"

Notice that according the warning, the children of Israel were vulnerable to forgetting the Lord when they failed to keep His word. It's the equivalent of moving away from God and leaning on your own understanding.

The other vulnerability was when everything was going right in their lives. They had plenty to eat, nice home, business was good, and they had money in the bank (metaphorically speaking). During seasons of plenty, it's easy to forget the source of it all! You forget where you came from and that it was the Lord who brought you this far.

Forgetting about the Lord leads to pride: "...then you say in your heart, 'My power and the might of my hand have gained me this wealth' (Deuteronomy 8:17). Wow - at this stage, you've gotten so far away from God that you look at your material possessions and think that you did it. This is the situation in which the scripture warns us in 1 Corinthians 10:12: "Therefore let him who thinks he stands take heed lest he fall."

So how do you take heed? Deuteronomy 8:18 gives us a clue: "And you shall remember the Lord your God, for it is He who gives you power to get wealth, that He may establish His covenant which He swore to your fathers, as it is this day."

"Remembering" and "Relationship" are the keys to avoid getting puffed up. To remember, I suggest you start a journal and start writing down all the blessings God imparts to you, at the moment they happen. In the journal, you give Him praise! Not only does it help you remember the Lord when times are good, it helps you stay encouraged when times are challenging. You see how God came through for you in the past and how He will do so in the future.

As for relationship, that means fellowshipping with the Lord everyday through regular prayer, praise, worship, and study of the Word. Seek His wisdom and strength in every circumstance. As you increase your dependence on God, you have no room for hot air.

As you empty yourself, you become filled with God. You are able to relate to other people out of humility and able to reflect the true image of our Father.

Speak the WORD

Speak this affirmation out loud as often as possible, based on this week's study:

> God, you are the source of everything I am and everything that I have. I am nothing without you. Empty me, Lord. Fill me with yourself so that I can be a true reflection of your Love to a hurting world. I acknowledge you in all my ways and I know that you will direct my path just as you promised.

Aim For Change

Read Deuteronomy 8:8-18 and then answer the following questions.

1. What was the warning given to the children of Israel?

2. What would cause the Israelites to forget the Lord?

3. What type of material possessions did the Lord say the Israelites would possess?

4. From which circumstances did the Lord deliver the Israelites from?

5. Why did the Lord say He took the Israelites through the wilderness?

6. When the Israelites became wealthy, to which attitude of heart were they vulnerable?

7. Think about your attitude regarding your Spiritual gifts and material possessions. Do you take the time to acknowledge God as the source? What is your daily relationship with the Lord? Take time to determine how you can pay closer attention to these areas. Failure to do so will impact your ability to love God and love others.

Week 6: Love Does Not Behave Rudely

Focus scripture

If you really fulfill the royal law according to the scripture, "You shall love your neighbor as yourself," you do well; but if you show partiality, you commit sin, and are convicted by the law as transgressors.

- James 2:8-9

Lesson Insight

In the bible, we are called royalty and holy: "But you are a chosen generation, a royal priesthood, a holy nation, His own special people, that you may proclaim the praises of Him who called you out of darkness into His marvelous light; (1 Peter 2:9)"

As royalty, clothed in the righteous robes of our Savior Christ Jesus, we are called to operate according to the royal law. Rudeness does not become us.

Rudeness is defined as being impolite, ill-mannered, crude, or disrespectful. Just the other day, I was checking at an online restaurant review when I came across one patron's description of another's behavior. Apparently, the restaurant was delayed in seating customers and according to the writer, the other customers didn't respond well:

> *Suddenly, a woman comes in from outside. Stout, shorter than me, and irate. She immediately starts whining, "Why can't we sit down?! We've been here forever! You're making us suffer outside in the fresh air! Oh gosh, how will I survive this night?!"*

> *Ok, ok, I used some generous hyperbole, but you get the picture. The hostess calmly tells the woman that they're having some troubles in the kitchen and*

can't seat anyone until they're all cleared up. If they can't serve them all menu items, they're not going to seat people and turn them down from their menu selections. It made sense to me and my boyfriend. But apparently we were the only ones that understood what was happening despite multiple iterations. This woman demands her Groupon (money she hasn't really spent yet) be extended because she can't endure any more of this. The manager comes out and extends the Groupons, but people still don't seem to understand that they're not seating for a legitimate reason. Instead, the furious crowd seems to think that this is a personal attack on them and they're just being downright mean here.

Here's where it gets good. As the crowd bum-rushed the hostess kiosk for their extensions, one woman stands on her tippy-toes and starts screaming, "The food is good, but not THAT good. The service here &*@!. I WILL NOT BE BACK HERE AND YOU SHOULDN'T EITHER. **WRITE YOUR REVIEWS, PEOPLE, WRITE YOUR REVIEWS!!**" And she proceeds to push people out of her way and leave the restaurant. The whole debacle was in poor taste on all of those

customers' parts, especially that
"reviewer" woman. I was disgusted by
the lack of manners and decency the
public showed.

Can you imagine what would have happened if
someone had followed the rude woman out
and spotted a big "Jesus" bumper sticker on
her car?

I shudder to think what would happen if I was
rude to a store clerk and then had that same
clerk visit our church - and see me sitting in a
pew! Don't you think that my rude behavior
would impact her opinion of my church and the
Lord?

I'd guess that many people are not in church
now because they were repelled by the un-
Christlike behavior of professed Christians.
Some of these might be members of your own
family.

That is why we Christians have to pay careful
attention to how we treat others, both in public
and in private. Jesus is the banner over our

lives and we represent Him in the world. The only "Jesus" someone may ever see is the Jesus in us!

The apostle James provides another example of rudeness in the church in James 2:1-4:

"My brethren, do not hold the faith of our Lord Jesus Christ, the Lord of glory, with partiality. For if there should come into your assembly a man with gold rings, in fine apparel, and there should also come in a poor man in filthy clothes, and you pay attention to the one wearing the fine clothes and say to him, 'You sit here in a good place,' and say to the poor man, 'You stand there,' or, 'Sit here at my footstool,' have you not shown partiality among yourselves, and become judges with evil thoughts?"

In this example, the person is showing kindness and consideration to the rich person but is rude to the poor man! I think about some people who may be rude routinely and excuse it by saying, "Well, that's just the way I am." I am tempted to ask those people, "Are you rude to your pastor? To your boss? Would you be rude to the President?"

If you treat those in authority with respect, but do not treat others with the same courtesy, then you are showing partiality, which is not pleasing to the Lord. Since you have the ability to control your attitude with these people of influence, then you have the ability to control it with those who can't do anything for you. You just have to want to be kind as an act of obedience to Christ. He will be faithful to help you if you but ask!

James 2:7 concludes: "If you really fulfill the royal law according to the scripture, 'You shall love your neighbor as yourself,' you do well; but if you show partiality, you commit sin, and are convicted by the law as transgressors."

If you have a tendency for rudeness, then remember who you are in Christ. As royalty, you don't have to prove anything to anyone. You can treat people well because you have an abundance of God's grace, His divine influence upon your heart to bear with them as He bears with you.

Speak the WORD

Speak this affirmation out loud as often as possible, based on this week's study:

> Lord, thank you for adopting me into your royal family. Because I am secure in your love for me, I can love others and treat them well. I live according to the royal law, which is my responsibility as the child of the King. Rudeness does not become royalty, so I treat others with kindness and consideration.

Aim For Change

Read 1 Peter 2:9 and James 2:1-4 and then answer the following questions.

1. In Peter 2:9, what are the people of God called?

2. According to the scripture, what are we called to do?

3. According to the scripture, what did God do for us?

4. According to James 2, what is the royal law?

5. In that chapter, what example did James give of a church member showing partiality?

6. How did James say that believers are judged who show partiality?

7. Think about your relationships with others. Are you routinely rude to them? How do you treat those in the service industry, your family? Ask the Lord in prayer to help you treat all people with the same kindness and consideration that He shows you.

Week 7: Love Does Not Seek Its Own

Focus scripture

Greater love has no one than this, than to lay down one's life for his friends.

- John 15:13

Lesson Insight

What greater role model of not seeking one's own than Jesus? For the three years of His Earthly ministry, the bible explains "how God anointed Jesus of Nazareth with the Holy Spirit and with power, who went about doing good and healing all who were oppressed by the devil, for God was with Him (Acts 10:38)."

All of the character traits of love are possible because God has anointed believers in Jesus with the Holy Spirit and power to do good! Anointed means "to choose by or as if by divine election." That means that you have the power to love people just as Jesus loved, in word and deed.

The bible doesn't say that Jesus only healed or did good on the days He felt like it or when it was convenient for Him. He was totally focused on doing what God called Him to do because He recognized that His purpose in living: "for the Son of Man has come to seek and to save that which was lost (Luke 19:10)."

What was lost? Mankind's ability to have a relationship with God. Remember in the Garden of Eden the first man, Adam, had a perfect relationship with God. He walked and talked with Him. God provided everything He needed, including a wife. However, the first couple sinned when they decided that God was withholding something desirable from them and that they could find satisfaction away from God.

It's the same mistake people make every day. Don't you see it in fruitless searches for money, sex, power, fame, and material goods? And yet, the real joy in life is in relationships, first with our heavenly Father and then with our Earthly family and friends.

I advise you to apply yourself to seeing everyone as **friends**. It doesn't mean that you share your innermost thoughts with everyone, but it does mean that you pray for and seek the best in the people you meet. Bring good news with you wherever you go. The best news is that they have the ability to have a relationship with God through Jesus Christ.

It may not always be easy, fun, or convenient to share the gospel with others. So when we take the time to tell someone how much God loves them or show them love when they are unlovable, you are laying down your life for them. It feels like death sometimes too, doesn't it? It feels like death when you hold yourself back from telling someone off who treated you unkindly.

And yet in doing so, we are presenting our bodies to the Lord so that He is glorified. He is pleased with it!

Let's take a look at Jesus and how he faced a situation, elevating His obedience to the Father's plan over his own temporary desire, beginning in Matthew 26:36-39:

"Then Jesus came with them to a place called Gethsemane, and said to the disciples, Sit here while I go and pray over there." And He took with Him Peter and the two sons of Zebedee, and He began to be sorrowful and deeply distressed. Then He said to them, "My soul is exceedingly sorrowful, even to death. Stay here and watch with Me."

Jesus knew that His hour had come and that Judas had betrayed Him. He knew that mankind needed redemption and it was the Father's plan that He be the sacrifice needed. He would cover mankind's sins with His own blood.

But this example shows us that even Jesus had moments of distress and sorrow! That is what makes Him a wonderful high priest for us. In His human body, scripture says that he was tempted in all the ways we are tempted; as shown in many instances in scripture like this one, He felt emotions as well. We can go to Him in confidence, knowing that he understands what we are going through.

Matthew 26:39 says, "He went a little farther and fell on His face, and prayed, saying, "O My Father, if it is possible, let this cup pass from Me; nevertheless, not as I will, but as You will."

This is an important turning point. Jesus sought the Father's face in prayer during the midst of his anguish. Do you go to God first when your emotions overwhelm you or do you get caught on an emotional merry-go-round? Let prayer be your first remedy for emotional distress.

In his prayer, Jesus asked the Father to let this cup (this responsibility for mankind's redemption) pass from Him if possible. Even in this, Jesus recognized that there is a higher plan at work in His situation. Notice He said, "*If it is possible*" which means He is recognizing the possibility that there is no other way to accomplish the Father's plan.

Then, He makes a statement that should guide our lives: "nevertheless, not as I will, but as You will."

So you see that Jesus submitted His own will to the Father's will. I once heard a definition of the word *submission* as "under the mission." That means recognizing that as a believer, you are not on this Earth to hang out. You are here on an assignment, on a mission.

In His statement, Jesus re-affirmed His desire to see the Father's will come to pass.

In our lives, we should daily seek to discover the Father's will for us. And then we should be mission-minded: Through the guidance of the Holy Spirit, we seek ways to show others the love with which Jesus loved us.

Hebrews 12:2 describes how Jesus empowers us, "looking unto Jesus, the author and finisher of our faith, who for the joy that was set before Him endured the cross, despising the shame, and has sat down at the right hand of the throne of God."

Even though Jesus experienced sorrow and distress in the Garden of Gethsemane, He went all the way to the cross and was crucified. Why? Because He loved us and in the Spirit, he was joyful seeing what His death and resurrection would accomplish: The ability for sinful man to be reconciled to a Holy God for those who would accept Jesus Christ as Savior and Lord.

James 3:13-17 gives us final direction concerning the self-seeking attitude:

"Who is wise and understanding among you? Let him show by good conduct that his works are done in the meekness of wisdom. But if you have bitter envy and self-seeking in your hearts, do not boast and lie against the truth. This wisdom does not descend from above, but is Earthly, sensual, demonic. For where envy and self-seeking exist, confusion and every evil thing are there. But the wisdom that is from above is first pure, then peaceable, gentle, willing to yield, full of mercy and good fruits, without partiality and without hypocrisy. Now the fruit of righteousness is sown in peace by those who make peace (James 3:13-17)."

Speak the WORD

Speak this affirmation out loud as often as possible, based on this week's study:

> Lord, I thank you that 'Nevertheless, not as I will but as You will' guides my life. I recognize when my attitude is self-seeking and immediately correct it through the empowerment of the Holy Spirit within me. My works are done in the meekness of wisdom and I glorify God in all my ways.

Aim For Change

Read Matthew 26:36-39 and James 3:13-17 then answer the following questions.

1. What emotions did Jesus experience in the Garden of Gethsemane?

2. What does this say about His role to us as our high priest?

3. When Jesus prayed, what did He ask of the Father?

4. In what way did Jesus submit His own will to the Father's will?

5. In James, how are envy and self-seeking described?

6. How is Godly wisdom described?

7. Think about the attitudes that guide your daily decisions. Do you seek God's will in prayer? In your dealings with others, are your motives self-seeking? If you need an adjustment in these areas then ask

the Lord in prayer to change your heart so that your desires line up with His desires.

Week 8: Love Is Not Provoked

Focus scripture

"This you know, my beloved brethren. But everyone must be quick to hear, slow to speak and slow to anger; for the anger of man does not achieve the righteousness of God."

- James 1:19-20

Lesson Insight

Provoke is defined as the ability to incite someone to do or feel strongly about something. When I hear the word, my first thought is provoking someone to anger. But in my research, I discovered that provoking someone can apply to any strong emotion or reaction.

Provoking can be particularly devastating in intimate relationships. After all, nobody knows your hot-buttons like your spouse! My husband knows exactly those things that irritate me. If he wanted to, he could push all of my buttons to get a rise out of me. And I could do the same thing to him if I wanted.

But he doesn't and I don't. We love each other and want to maintain peace in our household.

Now you might be thinking, "How can I avoid allowing other people to provoke me negatively?" I am glad you asked! One of the fruits of the Holy Spirit is self-control (see Galatians 5:22-23) so this maintaining emotional control is an achievable goal. But like any fruit, it takes time to develop.

A couple of years ago, the Holy Spirit gave me a revelation about the word "barometer." After looking it up, I discovered that a barometer measures pressure in the atmosphere. When the atmospheric pressure is high where you live, that means fair weather because the atmosphere is strong enough to resist stormy weather that is trying to come into your area.

But when the atmospheric pressure is low, storms can come in to your area because storms take the path of least resistance.

The key then to avoid allowing others to provoke you is to keep the atmospheric pressure inside yourself high through being filled with the Spirit. That way, when other people are pushing your hot-buttons, their negative influence can't get inside of you – after all, you are already filled!

Praying, meditating on the Father's word, and speaking it to yourself throughout the day keeps the spiritual pressure inside yourself high. These disciplines also inspire you to praise and worship God.

When praise and worship fills your heart, then you will know that your Spiritual atmospheric pressure is high enough to overcome any storms that come your way.

So think of your feelings as a barometer from now on. When you are full of the Spirit, love, joy, peace, patience, kindness, goodness, faithfulness, gentleness and self control reign within you.

But when you are spiritually low, you are habitually worried, troubled, fearful, doubtful, depressed, jealous, prone to anger, selfish, envious, and lack self control. During such times, it will be all too easy for the enemy to incite others to provoke you.

If you find yourself in a Spiritual low, then you need to retreat to the Father and build up the spiritual pressure inside yourself again so that you can resist the emotional storm.

This principle is illustrated vividly in the story of King David and Michal, his wife and daughter of Saul (2 Samuel 6:12-23). You may recall that Saul was the first king of Israel. However, due to his disobedience to God's commands, God removed the kingly anointing upon Saul and gave it to King David.

This incited jealousy and rage within Saul and he sought to kill David. Eventually, Saul met a tragic end and David was anointed King. One of the first things David did was set out to return the ark of Lord to its rightful place.

2 Samuel 6:16 says, "Now as the ark of the Lord came into the City of David, Michal, Saul's daughter, looked through a window and saw King David leaping and whirling before the Lord; and she despised him in her heart."

Even though David had done nothing wrong, perhaps Michal blamed him for her father's sad outcome. How different things might have been if Michal had been able to take her hurt and anger to the Lord and allowed Him to heal her and show her the true perspective of the situation. Perhaps she might have been praising the Lord with her husband and they leap and whirl in celebration together!

But instead, David was left to celebrate with the people by himself. 2 Samuel 6:20 records Michal's greeting to him when he got home: "How glorious was the king of Israel today, uncovering himself today in the eyes of the maids of his servants, as one of the base fellows shamelessly uncovers himself!"

Her greeting demonstrates disrespect and scorn, particularly grievous since she was talking to her own husband! In addition, it shows that Michal's heart was not with the Lord because she was more concerned with image rather than being delighted by David's unashamed demonstration of his joy in the Lord.

Because David was filled with Spirit, he was able to react to Michal not out of anger, but matter-of-factly and focus on the real issue at hand:

"So David said to Michal, 'It was before the Lord, who chose me instead of your father and all his house, to appoint me ruler over the people of the Lord, over Israel. Therefore I will play music before the Lord. And I will be even more undignified than this, and will be humble in my own sight. But as for the maidservants of whom you have spoken, by them I will be held in honor' (2 Samuel 6:21-22)."

David made no apologies for dancing before the Lord and in his response to Michal made it clear that he did not care how she perceived him, but he would continue to worship the Lord as the Spirit moved him. That is a great example for us; we should not allow other people's opinions to tempt us into violating our principles.

Scripture records that Michal never bore any children. Whether her barrenness was due to the Lord's divine judgment upon her or David's lack of physical intimacy with her, scripture doesn't say. But as Believers, we should always keep in mind that God is our defender so we do not have to react negatively when others treat us with disrespect. We let God judge them as He sees fit.

James 1:19-20 gives us a final guidance principle in our interaction with others: "This you know, my beloved brethren. But everyone must be quick to hear, slow to speak and slow to anger; for the anger of man does not achieve the righteousness of God."

Stay filled with the Spirit and be led by the Spirit so that you can accurately represent God to the people you meet. In that way, you will draw them to Jesus because they will see the difference in how you react to negative circumstances and want the peace that you have!

Speak the WORD

Speak this affirmation out loud as often as possible, based on this week's study:

> Lord, thank you for giving me a true picture of how my feelings should be used - as a Spiritual gauge. My aim is to keep myself filled with the Spirit through my prayers, praise, worship, and study of your Word so that I can avoid allowing others to provoke me. I want to accurately represent you to a hurting world and demonstrate the same love to them that you show to me. After all, you loved me when I was unlovable, so I will extend the same grace to them. Thank you, Father for loving me!

Aim For Change

Read 2 Samuel 6:12-22 and then answer the following questions.

1. What was the occasion that inspired David to dance before the Lord?

2. What did David do to show his joy to the people?

3. When David went home, what was his intention?

4. What greeting did he receive from his wife Michal instead?

5. In responding to Michal, do you think David showed the same attitude toward her as she showed to him? Why or why not?

6. What did David say he would do in response to Michal's criticism?

7. Think about your level of emotional control. Are you easily provoked to negative reactions when someone treats you poorly? What habits can you develop to keep yourself filled with the Spirit so

that you can accurately reflect God's love to others in spite of how they treat you?

Week 9: Love Thinks No Evil

Focus scripture

Finally, brethren, whatever things are true, whatever things are noble, whatever things are just, whatever things are pure, whatever things are lovely, whatever things are of good report, if there is any virtue and if there is anything praiseworthy—meditate on these things.

- Philippians 4:8

Lesson Insight

Wow, this love thing is getting deep isn't it? Not only does God want us to demonstrate love to others in our actions, but now He directs us to love them in our thoughts by refusing to think evil towards them.

"Now wait a minute," you might say, "Don't thoughts just appear randomly? How can I help it if an evil thought pops into my head?"

While some thoughts do appear in our head randomly based on our external circumstances or even the enemy trying to sow bad seed into our thinking, I believe that the "think no evil" principle is referring to those thoughts that we have habitually. I believe it is referring to our meditation.

When we meditate on something, we review it over and over in our minds. I think of a dog chewing on a juicy bone, trying to get every scrap of meat off of it, sucking the juices out of it until there is nothing left.

Now, I believe we should treat the word of God that way but too often we meditate on worldly things - worries about bills, fear of the future, how somebody treat us wrong. As we meditate on things that cause negative emotions, we tend to create external circumstances that harmonize with our internal environment.

That is why we are advised in Proverbs 4:23, "Keep your heart with all diligence, For out of it spring the issues of life." I think of the responsibility of keeping your heart is as serious as being a Goalkeeper (aka "Goalie") in a soccer game. The Goalie's job is to prevent the opposing team from scoring by intercepting the ball when they try to penetrate the goal net.

To be successful in thinking no evil towards others, you must be vigilant too in "casting down arguments and every high thing that exalts itself against the knowledge of God, bringing every thought into captivity to the obedience of Christ (2 Corinthians 10:5)."

It is impossible to take your thoughts captive if you don't know what the word of God says. When you know the word of God, then you can easily recognize thoughts that are contrary to it and reject them.

For example, if you are thinking about getting back at a person who has hurt you, then you recall and meditate on what the word of God says about the situation: "But I say to you, love your enemies, bless those who curse you, do good to those who hate you, and pray for those who spitefully use you and persecute you (Matthew 5:44)."

Instead of occupying your mind with evil thoughts of revenge, you instead fill them with praying for the person and seeking the Lord as to how you can show them love.

Our role model for this behavior is once again our Savior, Jesus. Matthew 12:22-30 shares the story of how He healed a demon-possessed man who was both blind and mute. But the Pharisees, the elite religious leaders of His day, thought evil of Him for doing so, and accused him of casting out demons by demonic power.

Matthew 12:22-27 records Jesus' reaction: "But Jesus knew their thoughts, and said to them: 'Every kingdom divided against itself is brought to desolation, and every city or house divided against itself will not stand. If Satan casts out Satan, he is divided against himself. How then will his kingdom stand? And if I cast out demons by Beelzebub, by whom do your sons cast them out? Therefore they shall be your judges."

Basically, Jesus was telling them that the demon inside of the man was doing Satan's work. It kept the man oppressed by rendering him blind and mute. What sense would it make for another demon (to which they attributed Jesus' power) to cast out the first demon - who was already doing the devil's work?

The word "devil" comes from the Greek word "diavolos" which means 'slanderer' or 'accuser'. If you allow slander or accusation to rule your mind, then mental strongholds are built that drive you to destructive behavior. It's like allowing the devil to set up housekeeping in your head!

However in this story, Jesus gave a great principle that all Believers should remember because it reinforces the principle of taking thoughts captive to the obedience of Christ: "But if I cast out demons by the Spirit of God, surely the kingdom of God has come upon you. Or how can one enter a strong man's house and plunder his goods, unless he first binds the strong man? And then he will plunder his house. He who is not with Me is against Me, and he who does not gather with Me scatters abroad."

As Believers, we are agents of the Kingdom of God. We are a part of the Great Commission to bring others to Christ. But Jesus is telling us that we will be unable to deliver people from Satan's grasp unless we first bind him in our own lives. And the first place we bind him is in our thinking because our thoughts impact our feelings and our feelings impact our actions.

The Pharisees failed to bind the "strong man" and their evil thoughts eventually drove them to seek ways to kill Jesus.

As additional insurance against evil thoughts, I recommend praying Psalm 19:14 regularly: "Let the words of my mouth and the meditation of my heart Be acceptable in Your sight, O Lord, my strength and my Redeemer."

Then, be diligent in meditating on the good news of the Gospel, getting every bit of nourishment from it that you can get to make yourself Spiritually strong. That way, you will be effective in plundering Satan's kingdom for God's glory!

Speak the WORD

Speak this affirmation out loud as often as possible, based on this week's study:

> Lord, I diligently apply myself to meditating on that which is true, noble, just, pure, lovely, good report, virtue and praiseworthy. The gospel is full of these things so I meditate on it! Thank you Lord for giving me the wisdom to guard my heart and take my thoughts captive to your obedience. As I do so, I am confident that I can do my utmost build your Kingdom.

Aim For Change

Read Matthew 12:22-30 and then answer the following questions.

1. In what condition was the man brought to Jesus?

2. What did Jesus do in response?

3. How did the multitudes react? How did the Pharisees react?

4. How did Jesus address their accusation that he was casting out demons by demonic power?

5. What did Jesus say one must do first before plundering a strong man's goods?

6. How did Jesus define those who are with Him versus those against Him?

7. Think about your ability to draw others to Christ. Have you been effective in this area? Consider the principle Jesus gave in his example of plundering the strong man's goods. If you are allowing evil thoughts to dominate your thinking, then you must first take those thoughts captive to the obedience of Christ through the power of God's word. Then, examine your life to determine if there are any areas in which Satan has

dominion and take them back through the power of the Holy Spirit.

Week 10: Love Does Not Rejoice in Iniquity

Focus scripture

When Jesus heard that, He said to them, "Those who are well have no need of a physician, but those who are sick. But go and learn what this means: 'I desire mercy and not sacrifice.' For I did not come to call the righteous, but sinners, to repentance."

- Matthew 9:12-13

Lesson Insight

When you learn of another person's sin, is your first response to rejoice or to grieve? While few of us would say "Yippee!" when hearing of another's transgressions, it's more common to feel a brief feeling of superiority as in "Well, at least I'm not *that bad*."

That's a form of rejoicing in iniquity. It causes a subtle form of self-righteousness, allowing us to elevate ourselves mentally above our sinning brother or sister. It's as if somewhere inside of us, we believe that God grades sin on a sliding scale.

But Isaiah 64:6 makes it plain: "But we are all like an unclean thing, And all our righteousness are like filthy rags; We all fade as a leaf, And our iniquities, like the wind, Have taken us away."

Notice the scripture says *all.* None of us will be able to stand before our Holy God at the throne of judgment based upon our own righteousness. Even the most seemingly sainted person has lied at least once in their lives! God's standard is perfection. No one has lived a perfectly sinless life but one: Our dear Savior Jesus Christ.

Jesus taught a parable about self-righteousness in Luke 18:9-14. "Also He spoke this parable to some who trusted in themselves that they were righteous, and despised others: "Two men went up to the temple to pray, one a Pharisee and the other a tax collector. The

Pharisee stood and prayed thus with himself, 'God, I thank You that I am not like other men—extortioners, unjust, adulterers, or even as this tax collector. I fast twice a week; I give tithes of all that I possess.'"

In the scripture, the audience that Jesus was speaking to were unloving and self-righteous. So the Pharisee in the story was meant to represent their attitude of false superiority.

Although the Pharisee was a religious man, can you hear the pride in his statements and rejoicing in naming the perceived sins of others? The Pharisee sounds like he is trusting in his own righteousness as his source of salvation. With a superior attitude, it is difficult to love others or show mercy to them. You forget that, "There but for the grace of God, go I!"

In contrast in the parable, Jesus gives the tax collector's view: "And the tax collector, standing afar off, would not so much as raise his eyes to heaven, but beat his breast, saying, 'God, be merciful to me a sinner!' I tell you, this man went down to his house justified rather than the other; for everyone who exalts himself will be humbled, and he who humbles himself will be exalted (verses 13-14)."

Now imagine the Pharisees' shock to hear Jesus commending a tax collector. Tax collectors were not held in high esteem in Jewish culture. They were viewed as traitors because they collected taxes from other Jews to give to the Romans. Many of them were known to be corrupt, collecting more money than what was required and pocketing the extra for themselves. As a result, many of them became wealthy in contrast to their poorer neighbors.

But the tax collector in the parable was commended for his attitude of heart towards God. He showed true repentance for his actions. He recognized his sin and asked for God's mercy. He understand that he could not justify himself; only God could. So he went to God ready to receive rather than thinking he already had it made.

In this parable as well as the scripture in Matthew 23:23, Jesus makes it clear how He viewed the Pharisees of His day: "Woe to you, scribes and Pharisees, hypocrites! For you pay tithe of mint and anise and cummin, and have neglected the weightier matters of the law: justice and mercy and faith. These you ought to have done, without leaving the others undone."

The lesson for us today is this: when we hear of a sinning brother or sister, our first thought should be one of humility and compassion. We should go to God in prayer not only interceding for them that the Lord return them to the right path, but also an occasion to ask God to examine our own hearts.

We recognize all too clear that our flesh nature has the ability to entice us into sin if we don't pay attention to our own thoughts and actions. We take 1 Corinthians 10:12 as a warning to us:"Therefore let him who thinks he stands take heed lest he fall."

Speak the WORD

Speak this affirmation out loud as often as possible, based on this week's study:

Lord, I thank you for Jesus! Without him, I have no right to a relationship with a holy God. I recognize that I am no better than any other person, subject to temptations of the flesh. So I take heed to my own walk with you and daily seek your face. I am only able to stand because you help me to stand.

Aim For Change

Read Isaiah 64:6, Luke 18:9-14, and Matthew 23:23. Then answer the following questions.

1. To what did Isaiah compare our righteousness and what did he say iniquity has the potential to do?

2. What attitude did the Pharisees that Jesus spoke to have toward others?

3. In the parable, in what way did the Pharisee rejoice in iniquity?

4. Why did the Pharisee believe he was righteous?

5. What attitude did the tax collector display during his prayers?

6. What traits did Jesus say were pleasing to God in the parable and in Matthew 23:23?

7. Think about your past reactions to hearing about another's transgressions. Do you have genuine compassion for them or is your first thought about your own superiority? Take a moment to meditate on where you were when you first came to Christ. In order to empathize with others and show compassion to them, we must **never** forget where we came from!

Week 11: Love Rejoices in the Truth

Focus scripture

I say to you that likewise there will be more joy in heaven over one sinner who repents than over ninety-nine just persons who need no repentance.

- Luke 15:7

Lesson Insight

In your "Aim for Change" assignment in the last lesson, I asked you to reflect on when you first came to believe in Jesus Christ as your Savior. Do you remember the joy and peace that flooded your heart at that time to know that your sins have been forgiven? You now had the ability to have a personal relationship with the God who created you and loved you enough to send his Son to die for your sins.

Rejoicing in the truth means that you rejoice whenever you see God's word and God's will come to pass on the Earth. Salvation is just the beginning of the believers reasons to rejoice. Recently, I meditated on three scriptures about joy:

"You have made known to me the ways of life; You will make me full of joy in Your presence (Acts 2:28).'

"You will show me the path of life; In Your presence is fullness of joy; At Your right hand are pleasures forevermore (Psalm 16:11)."

"Until now you have asked nothing in My name. Ask, and you will receive, that your joy may be full (John 16:24)."

Just in those three scriptures, I see four reasons to rejoice:

1. God's presence with us

2. God's wisdom in us.

3. God's direction for us.

4. God's blessings to us.

In response to the meditation previously, another scripture came to mind: "Blessed be the Lord, Who daily loads us with benefits, The God of our salvation! Selah (Psalm 68:19)."

I heard that "Selah" means to pause and think about that. Each of us as believers in Christ are loaded with benefits daily. That very thought makes me smile and just think about how good God is. Have you taken full advantage of your benefits package today?

God desires that all come to him to receive salvation in Jesus Christ, which makes them eligible to receive all the benefits he has for them. In the parable of the Prodigal Son, Jesus illustrated this desire.

Luke 15:11-16: "Then He said: 'A certain man had two sons. And the younger of them said to his father, 'Father, give me the portion of goods that falls to me.' So he divided to them his livelihood. And not many days after, the younger son gathered all together, journeyed to a far country, and there wasted his possessions with prodigal living. But when he had spent all, there arose a severe famine in that land, and he began to be in want. Then he went and joined himself to a citizen of that country, and he sent him into his fields to feed swine. And he would gladly have filled his stomach with the pods that the swine ate, and no one gave him anything."

I am sure that the young man had visions of how much fun it would be to live life on his own with no one telling him what to do. He apparently had everything that he needed from the goods that he received from his father to take care of his physical needs. But he lacked wisdom and the ability to see the future results of his present actions.

There's an old saying that goes "Sin will take you further than you want to go, keep you longer than you want to stay, and cost you more than you are willing to pay."

In this case, the young man's desire to live a wild lifestyle took him far from home, made him do degrading things to survive (feeding swine, which was an unclean animal in Jewish culture), and cost him all the money that he had.

Some would say that he deserved everything that he got! Perhaps he did. But isn't it wonderful that God has mercy on us and did not give us what we deserved? Scripture tells us that the wages of sin is death! But instead of giving us death for our sins, he gave us new life in Jesus Christ.

When we were saved, we all had a turning point just like the young man in the story:

Luke 15:17-19: "But when he came to himself, he said, 'How many of my father's hired servants have bread enough and to spare, and I perish with hunger! I will arise and go to my father, and will say to him, 'Father, I have sinned against heaven and before you, and I am no longer worthy to be called your son. Make me like one of your hired servants.'"

I love that statement, "but when he came to himself"! It was the moment when he realized that he was not sufficient within himself, but he needed salvation. While this story talks about physical salvation, a similar thing happened to us at the moment of our conversion.

The story continues: "And he arose and came to his father. But when he was still a great way off, his father saw him and had compassion, and ran and fell on his neck and kissed him. And the son said to him, 'Father, I have sinned against heaven and in your sight, and am no longer worthy to be called your son.' 'But the father said to his servants, 'Bring out the best robe and put it on him, and put a ring on his hand and sandals on his feet. And bring the fatted calf here and kill it, and let us eat and be merry; for this my son was dead and is alive again; he was lost and is found.' And they began to be merry (Luke 15:20-24)."

I love the father's reaction to his son's return. The son expressed genuine repentance and the father accepted him back without throwing his mistakes in his face. He freely forgave him and restored him to his position as son and heir.

In the later verses of the story, you learned that the older son was not happy about the younger son's return. He was angry at the father for accepting his brother back without question. His attitude was one of self-righteousness as we discussed in the previous lesson. In his mind, he felt that the younger son should be made to pay for his past transgressions.

But the father responded thusly, "And he said to him, 'Son, you are always with me, and all that I have is yours. It was right that we should make merry and be glad, for your brother was dead and is alive again, and was lost and is found (Luke 15:32).'"

The truth is that God doesn't love and forgive us because we are good, but because He is good! He gives us abundant grace that we can scarcely comprehend.

Meditating on this story makes me think about the wonderful song by John Newton "Amazing Grace:"

"Amazing Grace, how sweet the sound,

That saved a wretch like me.

I once was lost but now am found,

Was blind, but now I see."

God's grace toward us is the best reason to rejoice!

Speak the WORD

Speak this affirmation out loud as often as possible, based on this week's study:

> Lord, this is the day that you have made. I will rejoice and be glad in it. I thank you for your love, compassion, and the abundant grace you shower upon me. I celebrate the truths that you are always with me, your wisdom operates in me, you provide direction for me, and your blessings are available to me. Thank you God for loading me daily with benefits. I gratefully receive them all!

Aim For Change

Read Luke 15:11-31 and then answer the following questions.

1. What did the younger son request of the father?

2. What did the younger son do with what he received?

3. After he had spent all of his money, what was the situation the younger son found himself in?

4. In response, what did the younger son decide to do?

5. How did the father react when he saw his son?

6. What did the father give the younger son upon his return?

7. Think about your new life in Jesus Christ. The bible says that God loads us daily with benefits. Take a moment to reflect

upon the benefits you have received since becoming saved. How can you share the gospel with others you know so they too can receive the benefits of salvation?

Week 12: Love Bears All Things

Focus scripture

Brethren, if a man is overtaken in any trespass, you who are spiritual restore such a one in a spirit of gentleness, considering yourself lest you also be tempted. Bear one another's burdens, and so fulfill the law of Christ. For if anyone thinks himself to be something, when he is nothing, he deceives himself. But let each one examine his own work, and then he will have rejoicing in himself alone, and not in another. For each one shall bear his own load.

- Galatians 6:1-5

Lesson Insight

An important aspect of love is the ability to bear another's burdens. In order to do this, you must have empathy. Empathy is defined as the ability to identify with and understand another's situation, feelings, and motives.

I think when you love a person, you want to see them have God's best for them. And when you see them struggling, you want to do what you can to help, even if you can do nothing but provide a sympathetic ear. When you are dealing with a challenge, it is a great comfort to feel that you are not alone.

In our focus scripture, we are directed to cultivate a spirit of restoration whenever we encounter a person who is struggling with sin, rather than a spirit of "I told you so," superiority, or self-righteousness. We are told that we should consider ourselves and our own walk with Christ to be sure that we are not similarly tempted.

As story in Exodus illustrates beautifully the value of having others help you to bear your burdens:

Exodus 17:8-13 records the story of how the Israelites fought the Amalekites. Joshua was in charge of the Israelite army and Moses directed him to go out to battle while he was to stand on a hill with the rod of God in his hand. Joshua obeyed Moses command. Moses took his spot on the hill and took Aaron and Hur with him.

As Christians, isn't it good to know that we don't have to battle alone? That is why the Bible directs us not to forsake assembling together in the local church with other believers (see Hebrews 10:25). In this way, you can encourage others and receive encouragement yourself. In addition, through spiritual warfare we can accomplish far more with others than we can alone.

In Leviticus 26:8, the Israelites were promised "Five of you shall chase a hundred, and a hundred of you shall put ten thousand to flight; your enemies shall fall by the sword before you." I believe that the same principle applies spiritually. We can cause serious damage to Satan's kingdom when we come together in prayer, praise, worship, and study of God's word.

Let's continue the story: "And so it was, when Moses held up his hand, that Israel prevailed; and when he let down his hand, Amalek prevailed. But Moses' hands became heavy; so they took a stone and put it under him, and he sat on it. And Aaron and Hur supported his hands, one on one side, and the other on the other side; and his hands were steady until the going down of the sun. So Joshua defeated Amalek and his people with the edge of the sword."

Do you see how Aaron and Hur were able to see that Moses was tired and provided what he needed in order to rest and yet still fulfill his responsibility to provide spiritual support to Joshua in the battle? They stood by him and were willing to endure discomfort themselves in order to see God's will be done. Because of their able support of their leader, Israel prevailed that day.

That's what we all need to keep in mind when we see another Christian brother or sister struggling. We are all on the same team and we all want to accomplish the same purpose; we want to see God's will to be done on Earth as it is in heaven. Each of us was created for purpose and when one wins we all win!

We support others because we love them and most importantly because we love God.

Now I do have a word of caution concerning bearing another's burdens. Although the Bible clearly directs us to do this, we must never do it to the point of allowing another person to avoid the consequences of sin.

For example, suppose you have a friend who is clearly an alcoholic. This person continually gets drunk and you have advised him to seek help and remove the liquor cabinet from his home. But he has ignored your advice.

Yet, this same friend expects you to lend a sympathetic ear and to bail him out of jail when he gets arrested for driving under the influence. In that case, you're not bearing his burden but enabling him to continue indulging in destructive behavior.

In the focus scripture, we are told that we are to examine our own work, and to bear our own load. It would be different if this friend would admit that he was an alcoholic, sought help, and did everything possible to remove the temptation from his home.

You could assist him in bearing his load through keeping him accountable if he asks or even providing a ride to support group meetings if he needs transportation.

Do you see the difference? You are helping him to fulfill his God-directed responsibility to remain temperate in all things. If he is struggling with that responsibility, then a loving gesture is to help them with that. Keep in mind the example of Aaron and Hur supporting Moses. Your support should always be given when it helps fulfill kingdom purposes.

Speak the WORD

Speak this affirmation out loud as often as possible, based on this week's study:

> Lord, thank you for giving me an empathetic heart to be able to recognize and identify with another's feelings, situation, and motive. Thank you for giving me discernment to recognize when it is appropriate to bear another's burdens versus when it will be inappropriate because it is enabling destructive behavior in them. Thank you for giving me a kingdom mindset so that I can look past personal inconvenience to accomplish your purpose on this Earth.

Aim For Change

Read Exodus 17:8-16 and then answer the following questions.

1. What was Joshua's role in the battle against the Amalekites?

2. What was Moses' role in the battle against the Amalekites?

3. Who did Moses take with him?

4. What happened when Moses held up his hands? What happened when he let his hands down?

5. When Moses' hands became heavy, how did Aaron and Hur respond?

6. What was the end result of Aaron and Hur's support of Moses?

7. Think about your current relationships. Are you able to be empathetic to another's struggles? Do you provide support when needed to help others fulfill their God-given responsibilities?

Week 13: Love Believes All Things

Focus scripture

Jesus said to him, "If you can believe, all things are possible to him who believes."

- Mark 9:23

Lesson Insight

I think this lesson theme has the potential to be misleading; it says love believes all things and many interpretations have been written as to what it means. However, one thing is clear; it doesn't mean that you need to believe everything that you hear or read!

This is particularly true when it comes to information that contradicts our faith and our belief that Jesus Christ is the only way to God.

In fact, scripture tells us that we need to be discerning in this regard:

"Beloved, do not believe every spirit, but test the spirits, whether they are of God; because many false prophets have gone out into the world. By this you know the Spirit of God: Every spirit that confesses that Jesus Christ has come in the flesh is of God, and every spirit that does not confess that Jesus Christ has come in the flesh is not of God. And this is the spirit of the Antichrist, which you have heard was coming, and is now already in the world (1 John 4:1-3)."

I once had a visitor to my takebackyourtemple.com blog who read a negative review that I wrote about a secular book called "Women, Food, and God" in which I wrote that the title was misleading because in the book the author said that it didn't matter if the reader believes in one God, many gods, or even no God.

She commented on the blog that she was a minister's wife and that we as Christians should be open to all. She then asked the question, "Isn't that what Jesus said?"

I responded that although the Bible is clear that we should love our neighbors as ourselves, that doesn't mean that we should accept every doctrine that is preached to us. I gave her the scripture that I've shared previously from 1 John 4:1-3, and asked her if she could tell me where in the Bible that Jesus says that we should be open to all. I never received a response back.

That is why we have to read the Bible for ourselves. God's word must be our standard for truth and our "plumbline" by which all facts are evaluated.

In addition to being discerning about the facts that we choose to believe, I think we must be clear that we believe in the power of God to change hearts when we interact with others. And we must live out the fact that we believe that God's word is true. In this way, we help to draw others to believe in Jesus Christ.

In Mark 9:17-29, the Bible records one man's encounter with Jesus and his personal experience of his healing power:

"Then one of the crowd answered and said, 'Teacher, I brought You my son, who has a mute spirit. And wherever it seizes him, it throws him down; he foams at the mouth, gnashes his teeth, and becomes rigid. So I spoke to Your disciples, that they should cast it out, but they could not.' He answered him and said, 'O faithless generation, how long shall I be with you? How long shall I bear with you? Bring him to Me (verses 17-19).'"

In the story, it is clear that the man's son was suffering greatly. I am sure that he brought his son to the disciples with great expectation. What a disappointment to find that they could not help him!

But now, he was face-to-face with the master himself. When Jesus heard what happened, he lamented them as a faithless generation. I think of faith as the ability to see with your spiritual eyes that which God has promised. Faith is not needed where you can already see the thing that you are believing for. However it takes faith to believe God when he says, "But to you who fear My name The Sun of Righteousness shall arise With healing in His wings (Malachi 4:2);" — especially when you see a person so obviously sick right in front of you!

They brought the man's son to Jesus and when he saw Jesus, he immediately went into convulsions, an even more dramatic demonstration of his oppression.

Then Jesus asked the father a question: "How long has this been happening to him?"

The father answered, "From childhood. And often he has thrown him both into the fire and into the water to destroy him. But if You can do anything, have compassion on us and help us (verses 21-22)."

The father's last statement is very telling; notice that he says *but if* you can do anything. If you only strike those two little words from the sentence, you would have to perfect statement of faith!

Upon hearing this, Jesus gave us a great principle of faith that we should all take to heart: "If you can believe, all things are possible to him who believes."

You see, that is the thing that I believe this lesson is referring to. We believe in Jesus and we believe that his word is true.

In response to Jesus' the child's father said with tears, "Lord, I believe; help my unbelief (verse 24)!"

That is all that Jesus needed. I believe that he was able to see the man's heart and caught a glimpse of the man's vision of his son healed and whole. As a result, Jesus was able to cast out the deaf and dumb spirit and the son was healed.

The same power by which Jesus was able to cast out the demon is the same power that lives within each believer, which is the power of the Holy Spirit. So why do we see so few miracles and demonstrations of that power?

The disciples asked Jesus why they couldn't do the same thing that he did in healing the son. Jesus answered that the kind of spirit they were dealing with could only come out by prayer and fasting. Jesus had a regular disciplined spiritual life. I believe that if we desire to see God's power manifested in greater measure and set free those are bound, then it is necessary for us to decrease the world's influence on our minds and hearts and increase God's influence.

That means spending quiet time with him in prayer daily, studying the word and meditating on it to the point that it paints pictures inside of us as to what is possible to manifest. In that way, when we encounter others who are bound, we can say "It is not supposed to be this way" and be able to speak God's word into the situation with full confidence and belief, fully expecting it to come to pass just as God said:

""For as the rain comes down, and the snow from heaven,

And do not return there,

But water the Earth,

And make it bring forth and bud,

That it may give seed to the sower

And bread to the eater,

So shall My word be that goes forth from My mouth;

It shall not return to Me void,

But it shall accomplish what I please,

And it shall prosper in the thing for which I sent it (Isaiah 55:11)."

When we believe in greater measure the truth of God's word and in the power of his might, you will be able to show his love with powerful demonstrations that a hurting world cannot deny!

Speak the WORD

Speak this affirmation out loud as often as possible, based on this week's study:

Lord, I believe that your word is true and your ways are right. I believe all things connected to my faith in Jesus Christ, using your Word as my standard for truth. I do not believe every spirit, but test them as the bible directs. I believe that I can demonstrate your power in greater measure in my life to enable others to experience the transforming power of your love just as I have.

Aim For Change

Read Mark 9:17-29 and then answer the following questions.

1. Why did the man bring his son to Jesus?

2. What happened when the disciples tried to cast the spirit out?

3. When Jesus heard what happened, why do you think he said "O faithless generation"?

4. When the man told Jesus how long his son had the illness, what indicated his doubt?

5. What did Jesus say in response to the man?

6. When Jesus commanded the spirit to come out, what happened?

7. Think about your belief in God's word and his power. Do you have challenges in believing God's word is true and his ways are right? If so, ask the Lord in prayer to help your unbelief!

Week 14: Love Hopes All Things

Focus scripture

*Now hope does not disappoint,
because the love of God has been
poured out in our hearts by the
Holy Spirit who was given to us.*

- Romans 5:5

Lesson Insight

I never noticed this before, but in 1 Corinthians
13:13 the apostle Paul says "And now abide
faith, hope, love, these three; but the greatest
of these is love." What I never noticed is that
hope is placed in the same category as faith
and love!

I'm sure most of us have heard plenty of
sermons about love and faith, but I don't recall

hearing a sermon about hope in recent memory. What is hope? I think of hope as a deep desire in your heart mixed with expectation. The expectation part is very important; you can have a deep desire in your heart but secretly think that it will never happen. Unbelief kills hope.

However, believing God's ability to accomplish his purpose through you ignites your hope. You believe Jesus when he says that with God all things are possible.

Two scriptures in particular lead me to believe that God is the author of hope:

"For I know the thoughts that I think toward you, says the Lord, thoughts of peace and not of evil, to give you a future and a hope (Jeremiah 29:11).

"Delight yourself also in the Lord, And He shall give you the desires of your heart (Psalm 37:4)."

In the Jeremiah 29:11 scripture, God clearly says that he provides a future and hope to his children. This future for us was established before the foundation of the world! Unfortunately, we can delay that future or even derail it with ungodly choices.

However, the scripture Psalm 37:4 tells us how we can regain godly hope: it tells us that we should delight ourselves in the Lord and as we do so, he will provide the desires of our heart. Now my personal interpretation of this is not that he will give us everything that we want, but rather he will change our hearts so that our desires are in line with his perfect plan for us.

Here's how I see faith, hope, and love working together: first, we have to believe that God loves us. He loves us so much that he sent his only son to die for us. Once we believe in our hearts and confess with our mouth that Jesus is our Savior, we then have the ability to have a personal relationship with God. Through delighting ourselves in him and communicating with him every day, he begins to change our hearts. We begin to see things from his perspective and hope is birthed in our hearts.

With hope comes expectation, and with expectation faith. Hebrews 11:1 says, "Now faith is the substance of things hoped for, the evidence of things not seen." This scripture gives us a big clue as to how things are manifested in this life. The whole process is very creative! Think about how substances like Jell-O and Clay are molded. These things are formless at first, but put them into the mold and they take on the shape of that mold.

So I think when you hope for something, you are creating a mold for it. To bring it to pass, you need to fill it with the substance of faith. You have to believe that because you have that desire in your heart and through consistent fellowship with God, that desire is in line with his plan for you, then he will bring it to pass through you.

This sequence was illustrated in the life of Jesus. It started with love; scriptures tell us that God sent Jesus because he loved us. So God created the mold, the plan by which Jesus would be born, live, and the means by which he would die. In the Bible, Jesus is called "The Hope of Israel."

Now that the mold was created, faith had to fill it. Jesus was birthed through Mary because she had the faith to believe the message that the angel Gabriel told her. Throughout Jesus' life, he demonstrated faith as he sought to fulfill the father's will. Jesus' faith was powerful enough that he was able to restore sight to blinded eyes, made the lame walk, and cured countless diseases and raised people from the dead!

Today, Jesus is the reason for hope. Let's take a closer look at Romans 15:5-13, which illustrates how faith in Jesus, hope, and love work together in our relationships:

"Now may the God of patience and comfort grant you to be like-minded toward one another, according to Christ Jesus, that you may with one mind and one mouth glorify the God and Father of our Lord Jesus Christ. Therefore receive one another, just as Christ also received us, to the glory of God (Romans 15:5-7)."

In the above scripture, Paul exhorts us to unity. His prayer is that we as Christians be like-minded and glorify God with one mind and one mouth. That is the mold that God has created for how his church should operate.

Now in Romans 15:8-12, you see God's mold for how Jesus would fulfill ancient prophecies as well as reconcile Gentiles to God:

"Now I say that Jesus Christ has become a servant to the circumcision for the truth of God, to confirm the promises made to the fathers, and that the Gentiles might glorify God for His mercy, as it is written:

'For this reason I will confess to You among the Gentiles,

And sing to Your name.'

And again he says:

'Rejoice, O Gentiles, with His people!'

And again:

'Praise the Lord, all you Gentiles!

Laud Him, all you peoples!'

And again, Isaiah says:

'There shall be a root of Jesse;

And He who shall rise to reign over the Gentiles,

In Him the Gentiles shall hope.'"

Hallelujah! Doesn't reading that make you want to shout praise to the Lord? Most of us reading this Bible study would be classified as Gentiles. So you see that God already had a plan of redemption not only for Israel, but for us! Just as God's word said, he gave us hope and a future.

Let's end this lesson with Paul's final prayer in verse 13: "Now may the God of hope fill you with all joy and peace in believing, that you may abound in hope by the power of the Holy Spirit."

Paul exhorts us to hope; we should love others enough to hope the best for them. We should hope for and pray for their salvation. By faith, we should study the word and live it out in our lives so they can see God's power at work.

Now you might say, "What if I hope all of these things and they never happen?" Many people are afraid to hope because they are afraid of being disappointed. But I think disappointment only happens when you try to put a time limit on God. When things don't happen in the timeframe that you think they should, then you become disappointed.

I used to be like that, but then I saw an interview with a guest on a Christian program who was suffering from multiple sclerosis. Something she said has stayed with me until this day: "I am believing that God will heal me from this disease. However, I am leaving it up to Him as to whether he heals me on this side of glory or on the other side."

We have to recognize that God doesn't view time the way that we do. So we can hope, for example, that our loved ones get saved, but not have any expectation of the timeframe in which it will happen. The truth is, we may never see it happen in our lifetime. But we have to believe that because God placed that hope in our hearts that it will happen, even in our absence from this life.

We have to believe that this scripture is true: "Now hope does not disappoint, because the love of God has been poured out in our hearts by the Holy Spirit who was given to us (Romans 5:5)."

Speak the WORD

Speak this affirmation out loud as often as possible, based on this week's study:

> Lord, thank you that you love me enough to give me hope and a future. I dedicate myself to spending time with you so that you give me the desires of my heart, which are in harmony with your desires for me. I rely on the Holy Spirit's wisdom to show me how to bring those desires into reality. By faith, I walk them out and I see your will done on Earth as it is in heaven.

Aim For Change

Read Romans 15:5-13 and then answer the following questions.

1. What character traits did Paul use to describe God?

2. What was Paul's exhortation to the believers in Rome to encourage unity?

3. For what purpose was unity necessary?

4. Why did Paul say that Jesus had been sent as a servant?

5. When the Gentiles received the Lord, what did the prophecy say what would be their response?

6. What was Paul's final prayer for the Romans?

7. Think about your relationship with Jesus Christ. Scripture says that he is the reason for our hope. If you have any areas in which you feel that you have

lost hope, meditate on Jesus, the author and finisher of your faith. Dedicate yourself to spending time in prayer so that you can regain your confidence that if you have hope in your heart, that God put it there and as such, he will bring it to pass in your life as you walk by faith.

Week 15: Love Endures All Things

Focus scripture

And let us not grow weary while doing good, for in due season we shall reap if we do not lose heart.

- Galatians 6:9

Lesson Insight

Up until this point, the scriptures that we have read have shown us how to operate in love towards people. The quality of our lives really boils down to the quality of our relationships. We are called to pursue peace with all men and when it comes to our Christian brothers and sisters, we are told not to forsake assembling with them.

However, in 2 Thessalonians 3:6-15 we are given clear direction as to when we are to withdraw from an association with a fellow Christian:

"But we command you, brethren, in the name of our Lord Jesus Christ, that you withdraw from every brother who walks disorderly and not according to the tradition which he received from us. For you yourselves know how you ought to follow us, for we were not disorderly among you; nor did we eat anyone's bread free of charge, but worked with labor and toil night and day, that we might not be a burden to any of you, not because we do not have authority, but to make ourselves an example of how you should follow us. For even when we were with you, we commanded you this: If anyone will not work, neither shall he eat (2 Thessalonians 3:6-10)."

To be disorderly means to behave without any boundaries. You just do whatever you want to do without any regard to how it affects others. In addition, in Paul's example, it means to be preoccupied with worldly busyness rather than being occupied with God's business.

I once heard a motivational speaker say, "If you want to know where you are headed, check out your friends." It is true that the people that we tend to associate with most often have the power to impact how we behave and what we come to think of as acceptable.

Returning to the story, Paul led by example. He conducted himself in a godly manner. Because he was concerned about others, he worked to help provide for his own living to avoid burdening his hosts. He exhorted others to do their fair share as well.

Paul continued his direction concerning disorderly believers in verses 11-12: "For we hear that there are some who walk among you in a disorderly manner, not working at all, but are busybodies. Now those who are such we command and exhort through our Lord Jesus Christ that they work in quietness and eat their own bread."

What does it mean to be a busybody? It means that you busy yourself with gossip and/or inserting yourself into other people's business. Because you do that, you waste valuable time that could be spent on doing the work that God has called you to do! But Paul tells such people that they should turn their attention to their own work. After all, God is not going to judge you by what someone else is doing, but by what you did with the resources that he has given you.

Lastly, in verses 13-15, Paul gives other directions about this issue: "But as for you, brethren, do not grow weary in doing good. And if anyone does not obey our word in this epistle, note that person and do not keep company with him, that he may be ashamed. Yet do not count him as an enemy, but admonish him as a brother."

In these verses, Paul exhorts us not grow weary in doing good. In the Bible we are promised that we will reap if we do not faint and that God is the source of our strength. So, we can help ensure our spiritual strength by spending time with God in prayer, praise, worship, and study of his word.

In addition, we can renew our strength by fanning the flames of hope in our hearts. We can meditate on those things that we are hoping for, visualizing them coming to pass. When we can see the results of what we are hoping for, we are more diligent in working for them in faith.

Finally, Paul tells us that if there are those around you who do not live according to God's word (Christian brothers and sisters), then you are not to keep company with them. But you are to tell them the truth in love as the Holy Spirit directs you.

The operative word is **love**. So you endure in prayer for them, and continue to hope and belief that God's will shall be manifested in their lives. While you are hoping for them, you are continuing to be rooted and built up in God's love yourself so that it has full expression in the way that you live and love others.

Speak the WORD

Speak this affirmation out loud as often as possible, based on this week's study:

Lord, thank you for giving me your word so that I may live an orderly life that pleases you. I occupy my days in fellowship with you and in accomplishing your business no matter the role to which I am called. I strive to live a life that serves as an example for my fellow Christian brothers and sisters. If I see a Christian brother or sister walking disorderly, I tell them the truth in love as the Holy Spirit directs.

Aim For Change

Read 2 Thessalonians 3:6-15 and then answer the following questions.

1. What do you consider to be disorderly behavior?

2. Why do you think Paul advised believers to withdraw from those who are disorderly?

3. How did Paul demonstrate orderly behavior?

4. What disorderly behavior did Paul specifically describe in the letter?

5. What was Paul's exhortation to those engaged in disorderly behavior?

6. What was Paul's exhortation for those who had to deal with another's disorderly behavior?

7. Think about your current relationships. If you have Christian brothers and sisters who engage in disorderly behavior, how can you show love to them while addressing that behavior?

Study Summary: Love Never Fails

In the *Fifteen Shades of Love* bible study, you were taught how love should be expressed according to God's word. The love God has for his people is *Agape* love, which is a Greek word translated as "a commitment of the will to cherish and uphold another." This is loving someone regardless of how you feel; it is loving someone apart from how they treat you.

In order to love others, you must first be able to receive God's love for you. Only then can you love yourself and be able to love them out of the overflow.

Love never fails because God is love - and He never fails!

Points to Remember

- Love is long-suffering. Remind yourself that love is a commitment of the will, not a commitment of the feel. Make up your mind to do what pleases God, no matter what. Resolve to wait patiently for people, praying for them and trusting that God will continue to work on them. Use God's long-suffering with you as a role-model.

- Love is kind. To be kind to someone is to be courteous, gentle, and gracious. It is treating other people with respect. The principle of the Golden Rule is to "do unto others as you *would have them do* unto you," not "do unto others as *they are doing* unto you.

- Love does not envy. Envy causes you to resent the other person and that resentment will affect how you treat them. Instead, we are exhorted to be content with the things we have. Contentment means that you maintain a state of peaceful happiness with what you have now, even if you desire more for the future. You truly enjoy what you have, recognizing that it all comes to you from God's generous hand.

- Love does not parade itself. As a disciple of Christ, your motive for your actions is not "look at me," but "look at Him." We want others to see the Christ in us so that they too will accept him as their Savior and be drawn into a personal relationship with Him.

- Love is not puffed up. A major danger of being puffed up is forgetting that the Lord is the source of everything you are and everything you have. This creates separation from God and, because you see yourself as higher than others, it would negatively impact your ability to love them. However, the closer you cling to God, the more you'll be able to love others the way He loves you. You'll be learning from the Master!

- Love is not rude. We Christians have to pay careful attention to how we treat others, both in public and in private. Jesus is the banner over our lives and we represent Him in the world. The only "Jesus" someone may ever see is the Jesus in us!

- Love does not seek its own. All of the character traits of love are possible because God has anointed believers in Jesus with the Holy Spirit and power to do good! Anointed means "to choose by or as if by divine election." That means that you have the power to love people just as Jesus loved, in word and deed.

- Love is not provoked. The key to avoid allowing others to provoke you is to keep the atmospheric pressure inside yourself high through being filled with the Spirit. That way, when other people are pushing your hot-buttons, their negative influence can't get inside of you – after all, you are already filled!

- Love thinks no evil. To be successful in not thinking evil of others, you must be vigilant in "casting down arguments and every high thing that exalts itself against the knowledge of God, bringing every thought into captivity to the obedience of Christ (2 Corinthians 10:5)." It is impossible to take your thoughts captive if you don't know what the word of God says. When you know the word of God, then you can easily recognize thoughts that are contrary to it and reject them.

- Love does not rejoice in iniquity. When you hear of a sinning Christian and you feel superiority and self-righteousness, that is a form of rejoicing in iniquity. It allows you to elevate yourself mentally above them. Instead, God calls you to humility and compassion. You should go to God in prayer not only interceding for them that the Lord return them to the right path, but also an occasion to ask God to examine your own heart, lest you be similarly tempted.

- Love rejoices in the truth. Rejoicing in the truth means that you rejoice whenever you see God's word and God's will come to pass on the Earth. Salvation is just the beginning of the believers reasons to rejoice.

- Love bears all things. An important aspect of love is the ability to bear another's burdens. In order to do this, you must have empathy. When you love a person, you want to see them have God's best for them and when you see them struggling, you want to do what you can to help, even if you can do nothing but provide a sympathetic ear.

- Love believes all things. You believe all things connected to your faith in Jesus Christ as written in the bible. You also must be clear that you believe in the power of God to change hearts when you interact with others. In this way, you help to draw others to believe in Jesus Christ.

- Love hopes all things. Believing God's ability to accomplish his purpose through you ignites your hope. You believe Jesus when he says that with God all things are possible. Scripture tells you that you should delight yourself in the Lord and as you do so, he will provide the desires of your heart. Through your relationship with him, he will change your heart so that your desires are in line with his perfect plan for you.

- Love endures all things. When you encounter a disorderly Christian brother or sister, you limit your association with them but you do not weary in doing good. You endure in prayer for them, and continue to hope and believe that God's will is destined to be manifested in their lives. While you are hoping for them, you are continuing to be rooted and built up in God's love for you so that it has full expression in the way that you live and love others.

About the Author

"Just wanted to again thank you for sharing your unique and engaging presentation to help us take back our temples! You were truly a blessing and I know that many were enlightened by what you shared."

- Danese Turner, Turner Chapel AME, Marietta GA

Kimberly Taylor is the creator of Takebackyourtemple.com, a website that inspires Christians to Spiritual, emotional, and physical health. She is the author of the ebook *Take Back Your Temple* and the books *The Weight Loss Scriptures, God's Word is Food*, and many others.

Once 240 pounds and a size 22, Kim lost 85 pounds through renewing her mind and taking action upon God's word. Her experience led her to establish the **Take Back Your Temple** website. "Take Back Your Temple" is a prayer that asks God to take control of your body and your life so He can use them for His purpose and agenda.

Kim's weight loss success story has been featured on CBN's *The 700 Club,* and in *Prevention Magazine*, *Essence Magazine*, *Charisma Magazine* and many other magazines and newspapers. She has also been interviewed on various radio programs.

Kim exhorts people of faith to become good stewards of all the resources God has given to them, including time, money, talents, and physical health. "I am passionate about empowering others to adopt healthy lifestyles so they can fulfill their God-given purpose," she says.

"My dream is for God's people to stand apart because we are healthy, prosperous and living the abundant life to which we are called. I want non-believers to look at us and want what we have: Spiritual, mental, and physical wholeness. Then when they ask us what we are doing differently, we can tell them about Jesus, the author and finisher of our faith."

Stay Connected

You can stay connected with Kimberly Taylor through the following channels:

Amazon Author Page

You can learn about all of Kimberly Taylor's books and eBooks available on Amazon.com at one convenient location: **https://www.amazon.com/author/kimberlyytaylor**

Take Back Your Temple website

Kimberly's website, **www.takebackyourtemple.com/** shares her testimony of deliverance from emotional overeating through the change God made in her heart and mind. Hundreds of free articles on the website encourage other Christians on the road to Spiritual, emotional, and physical health.

Facebook

You can connect with Kimberly on Facebook at
http://www.facebook.com/takebackyourt emple. She also moderates a secret Facebook support group comprised of believers who struggle with emotional eating and are working to change their health. Details on how to join the group are available at *takebackyourtemple.com*.

Twitter

Follow Kimberly on Twitter at
twitter.com/tbytkimberly

Pinterest

You can view Kim's Pinterest boards at
http://pinterest.com/tbyt/

All paperback versions of the *Bible Study for Women* series were published through **StartYourBook.org**.

www.ingramcontent.com/pod-product-compliance
Lightning Source LLC
Chambersburg PA
CBHW071533040426
42452CB00008B/996